LIVING COLOR

WRITTEN AND ILLUSTRATED BY
STEVE JENKINS

HOUGHTON MIFFLIN HARCOURT

BOSTON   NEW YORK

R ed frogs, blue spiders, yellow snakes, green birds, orange fish, purple snails, pink armadillos — animals can be surprisingly colorful. Like all living things, bright or dull, these creatures try to survive in a world that can be difficult and dangerous. If an animal is very colorful, it is likely that its brilliant skin, scales, or feathers somehow help it stay alive. This book takes a look at color in the animal world and some of the ingenious ways it is used. At the back of the book you can read more about animal colors and find additional information about the creatures shown — how big they are, where they live, what they eat, and more.

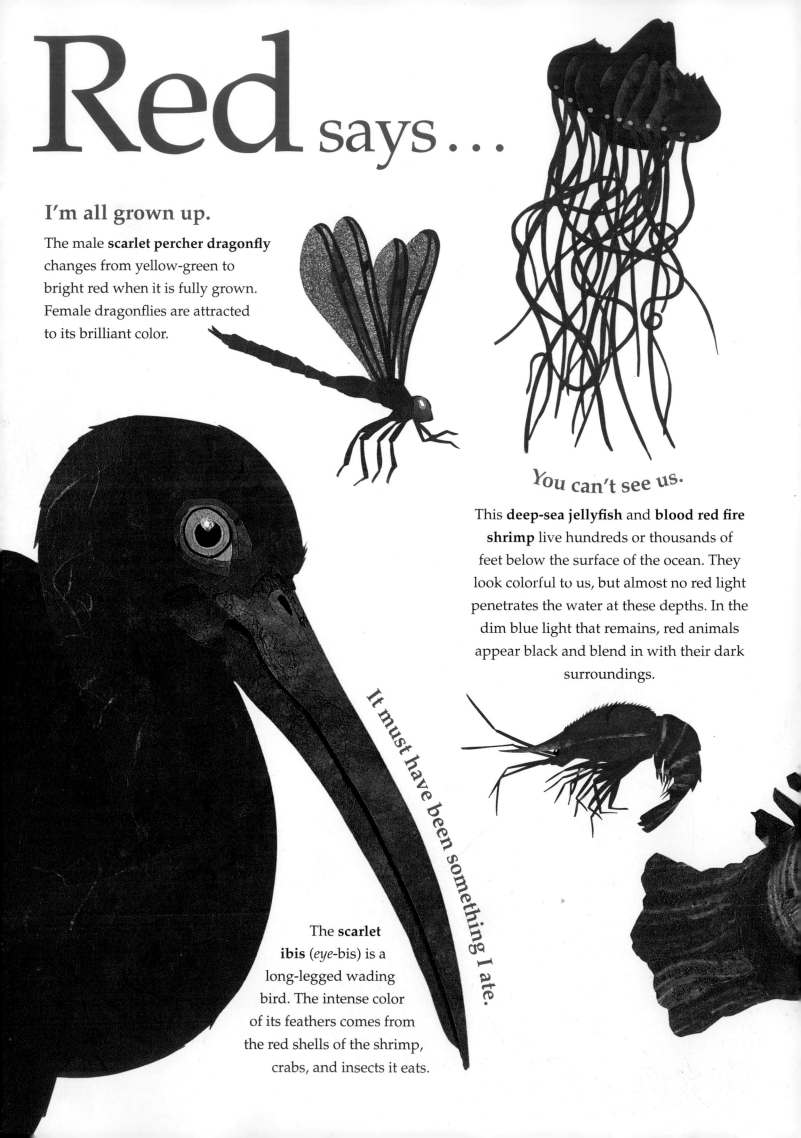

Red says...

I'm all grown up.

The male **scarlet percher dragonfly** changes from yellow-green to bright red when it is fully grown. Female dragonflies are attracted to its brilliant color.

You can't see us.

This **deep-sea jellyfish** and **blood red fire shrimp** live hundreds or thousands of feet below the surface of the ocean. They look colorful to us, but almost no red light penetrates the water at these depths. In the dim blue light that remains, red animals appear black and blend in with their dark surroundings.

It must have been something I ate.

The **scarlet ibis** (*eye*-bis) is a long-legged wading bird. The intense color of its feathers comes from the red shells of the shrimp, crabs, and insects it eats.

Don't even think about it.

The bright color of the **Malaysian cherry-red centipede,** like that of many poisonous animals, warns predators that it is dangerous and not good to eat. This centipede can also give a nasty bite with its venomous pincers.

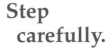

This is *my* space.

The male **hooded seal** marks its territory — and tries to impress female seals — by inflating a sac of loose skin that hangs from its left nostril, blowing it up like a big red balloon.

Step carefully.

The **stonefish** is the most poisonous fish in the world. It lives in shallow tropical seas and looks like a lumpy rock or piece of coral as it lies quietly on the ocean floor. Along its back are thirteen sharp, venom-filled spines that protect it from predators. A careless swimmer who steps on a stonefish receives a very painful stab and can die without medical treatment.

I look dangerous.

Despite its name, the **flame scallop** is actually a kind of clam. The brilliant color of its tentacles comes from the tiny plants and animals it filters out of the seawater. The flame scallop is harmless, but its tentacles look like those of a poisonous sea anemone.

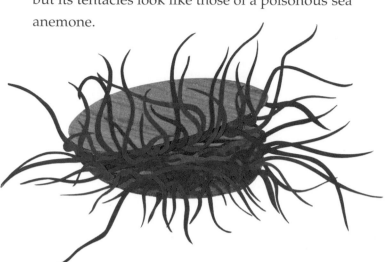

Hey – it's me.

The **'i'iwi** (ee-*ee*-wee) is a kind of honeycreeper, a group of birds that live in the tropics. The 'i'iwi is found in Hawaii and drinks flower nectar with its long curved beak. Many different kinds, or species, of honeycreeper live in the same forest. The distinctive red and black plumage of this bird helps 'i'iwis identify each other.

I'm the boss.

White uakaris (wah-*car*-ees) have only a little hair on their bright red faces. These South American monkeys live in large troops, each group of monkeys led by a dominant male. The monkey in charge always has the most intensely colored red face.

The skin of the **red salamander,** like that of many amphibians, is poisonous. Its bright color makes it easy to spot on the dark forest floor and warns predators to leave it alone.

You've got a little problem.

A **harvest mite larva** (its newly hatched form) is also called a chigger. It is tiny — smaller than the period at the end of this sentence. The chigger is a parasite, feeding on the skin of animals and humans. Its saliva dissolves the skin of its host so the chigger can slurp it up. An infestation of chiggers causes intense itching and can be very unpleasant. The bright red color of these eight-legged creatures warns predators that they are toxic and bad-tasting. An adult chigger looks like a little red spider. It feeds on plants and is harmless to humans.

I taste terrible …

… and I stink.

The **shield bug** also uses color to warn away birds and other predators. If threatened, it can release a foul-smelling chemical from a gland in its rear end.

The mouth of a baby **crow** is bright red inside. This color is a signal — it tells the mother and father crows that their babies are hungry and shows them where to put the food that they have brought back to the nest.

Put the food right here.

Red

Blue says…

The tiny **poison dart frog** eats ants, and the toxins these insects contain accumulate in the frog's body. This gentle amphibian does not attack humans, but the skin of one frog contains enough poison to kill dozens of people. Native hunters in the jungles of South America rub the tips of their arrows and darts on the frogs' skin.

Don't touch!

Look at me!

The male **hyacinth macaw** (*hi*-ah-sinth muh-*caw*), the largest of the parrots, displays its bright blue feathers to attract a mate. The same intense blue color makes this bird difficult for hawks and eagles to spot as the macaw wings its way through the cool, dappled light of the rain forest.

The **cleaner wrasse** (*rass*) doesn't hide when a bigger fish approaches. Potential predators recognize the bright color and distinct markings of the wrasse and do not eat it. The wrasse has a special relationship with these bigger fish. It cleans them by eating parasites that live on their skin and gills.

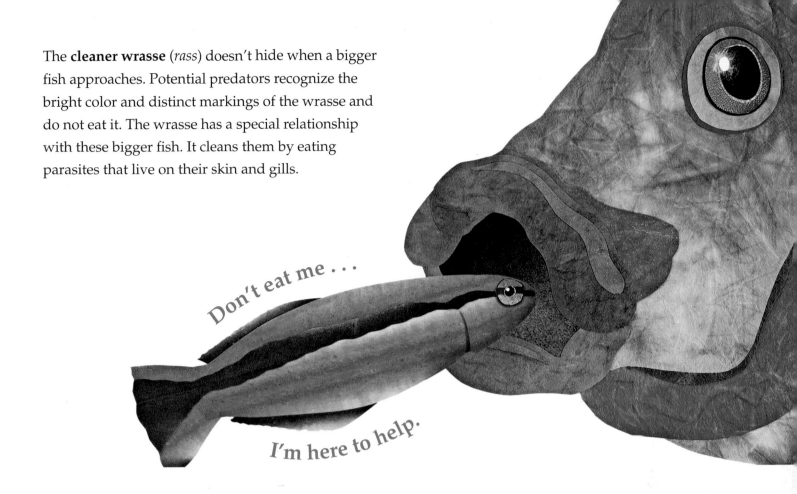

Don't eat me . . .

I'm here to help.

The wings of the **blue morpho butterfly** are dull brown on one side and an intense blue on the other. This butterfly can open its wings wide to show off its brilliant color and attract a mate. As it flits through the dappled light of the jungle, opening and closing its wings, the blue morpho seems to appear, disappear, then appear again in a new location.

I'm a mystery.

The **robin**, a familiar backyard bird, is famous for its beautiful blue eggs. Does this color protect the eggs by making them difficult to see in the shadows of a nest? Perhaps. The eggs of many birds are colored because white eggs are easier for a predator to spot. Why robins' eggs are such an extraordinary shade of blue, however, no one really knows.

Now you see me,

now you don't.

The **Portuguese man-of-war** appears to be a large jellyfish, but it is really a colony of thousands of smaller animals called polyps (*pol*-ips). Named after an eighteenth-century sailing ship, the man-of-war drifts on the surface of the sea, pushed along by the wind. It snares fish and other small animals with long, poisonous tentacles that are hard to see in the blue water. A transparent blue body helps keep it hidden from sea turtles that find it tasty.

You can look right through me.

Pretty poison.

The **cobalt blue tarantula** is a jewel-like metallic blue. Its color seems to change as it moves, and it looks almost black from some angles. It is quick and aggressive, and sports a pair of poisonous fangs. This spider's color helps camouflage it as it scurries about in the shadows of the forest floor. Its intense blue coloration, like the bright colors of many dangerous animals, may also serve as a warning to predators.

Surprise!

The **blue-winged grasshopper** is a dull gray color until it suddenly opens its wings wide and reveals two bright blue patches. This sudden flash of color can startle an attacker and give the grasshopper a chance to escape.

When he wants to impress a female, the male **blue bird of paradise** hangs upside down, spreads out his long blue feathers, sways gently back and forth, and coos a soft song. There are many different bird of paradise species, each with its own bright colors and patterns. Besides providing a striking display, the blue plumage of these birds helps them find others of their kind.

I'm the one.

Didn't expect that, did you?

The **blue-tongued skink,** an Australian lizard, startles attackers by suddenly thrusting out its huge, shockingly blue tongue.

Made you look.

Another lizard, the **blue-tailed skink,** uses color in a different way. When in danger, it twitches its bright blue tail. If a predator grabs the lizard's tail instead of its body, the tail breaks off and continues to twitch. The lizard runs away and eventually grows a new tail.

Blue

Yellow says...

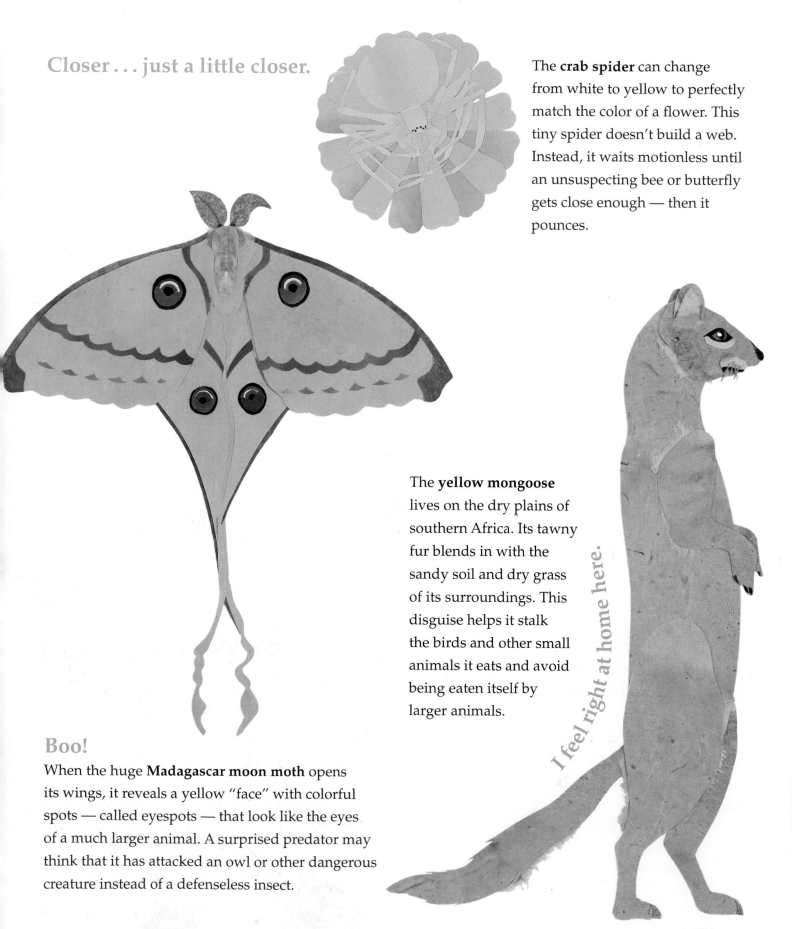

Closer... just a little closer.

The **crab spider** can change from white to yellow to perfectly match the color of a flower. This tiny spider doesn't build a web. Instead, it waits motionless until an unsuspecting bee or butterfly gets close enough — then it pounces.

The **yellow mongoose** lives on the dry plains of southern Africa. Its tawny fur blends in with the sandy soil and dry grass of its surroundings. This disguise helps it stalk the birds and other small animals it eats and avoid being eaten itself by larger animals.

I feel right at home here.

Boo!

When the huge **Madagascar moon moth** opens its wings, it reveals a yellow "face" with colorful spots — called eyespots — that look like the eyes of a much larger animal. A surprised predator may think that it has attacked an owl or other dangerous creature instead of a defenseless insect.

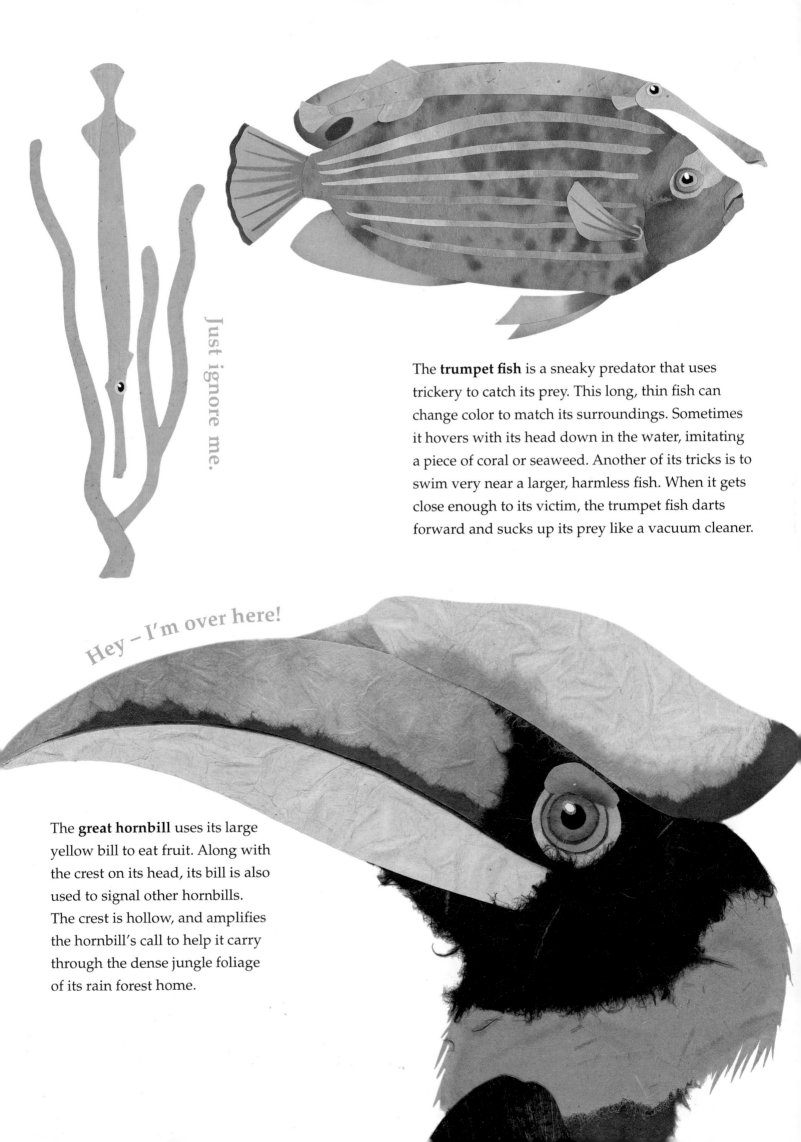

Just ignore me.

The **trumpet fish** is a sneaky predator that uses trickery to catch its prey. This long, thin fish can change color to match its surroundings. Sometimes it hovers with its head down in the water, imitating a piece of coral or seaweed. Another of its tricks is to swim very near a larger, harmless fish. When it gets close enough to its victim, the trumpet fish darts forward and sucks up its prey like a vacuum cleaner.

Hey – I'm over here!

The **great hornbill** uses its large yellow bill to eat fruit. Along with the crest on its head, its bill is also used to signal other hornbills. The crest is hollow, and amplifies the hornbill's call to help it carry through the dense jungle foliage of its rain forest home.

The deadly **eyelash viper** of Central America looks as if it would be hard to miss. Curled up among the colorful yellow fruit and flowers of the jungle, however, it can be perfectly camouflaged. When it's not lying in wait to ambush prey, the intense color of this poisonous snake warns other animals that it is armed and dangerous.

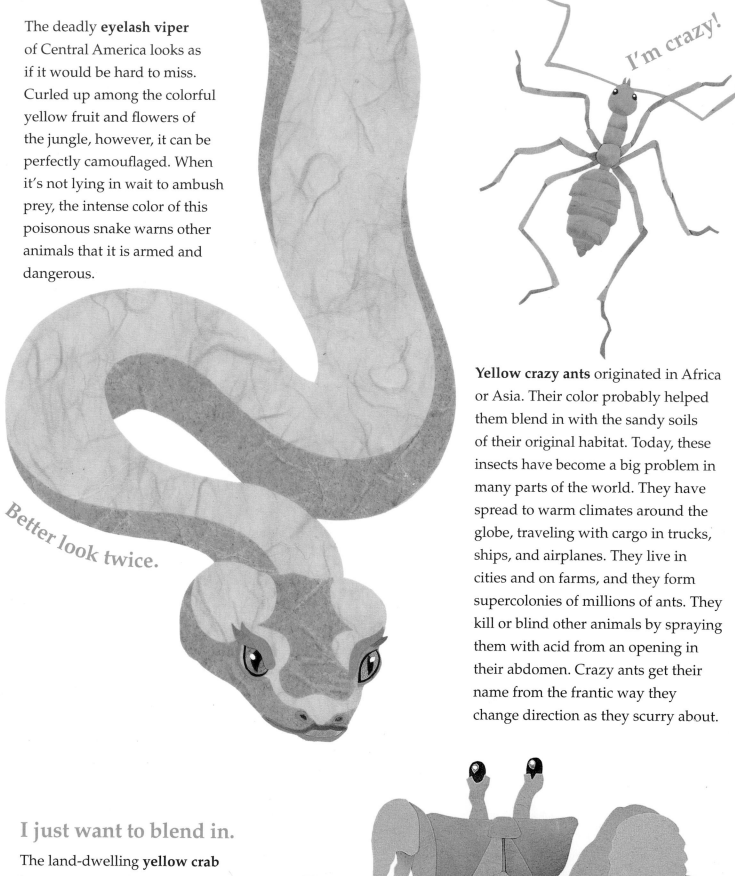

Better look twice.

I'm crazy!

Yellow crazy ants originated in Africa or Asia. Their color probably helped them blend in with the sandy soils of their original habitat. Today, these insects have become a big problem in many parts of the world. They have spread to warm climates around the globe, traveling with cargo in trucks, ships, and airplanes. They live in cities and on farms, and they form supercolonies of millions of ants. They kill or blind other animals by spraying them with acid from an opening in their abdomen. Crazy ants get their name from the frantic way they change direction as they scurry about.

I just want to blend in.

The land-dwelling **yellow crab** lives on tropical islands and shorelines. Its color makes it difficult to spot as it scuttles about among the dried leaves and plant litter of the forest floor.

Yellow

Yecch!

The bright color of this **ladybird beetle,** also called a ladybug, tells birds and other predators that it tastes really bad. These familiar insects can be found in yellow, orange, or red, with a varying number of black spots.

Do you find me . . . attractive?

The male **American goldfinch,** or wild canary, turns bright yellow during its mating season. Intensely colored feathers are a sign of good health. The female prefers a healthy-looking mate, since he will be more likely to survive and help raise their chicks.

I'm complicated.

The **common cuttlefish** is a master of color change. It can turn from its normal brownish color to green (or blue, pink, or purple) in seconds. When a cuttlefish is excited, waves of color wash over its body. The cuttlefish can "hypnotize" shrimp and small fish with a mesmerizing display of changing colors. When the small animals stop to stare, the cuttlefish grabs them with its long tentacles. Cuttlefish can also change color to match their surroundings.

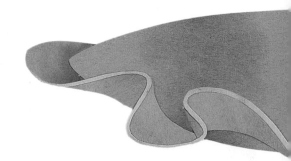

Green says...

Animal or vegetable?

The **leaf insect** has evolved to look just like its surroundings. When it is sitting still, it can look exactly like part of a plant. Different kinds of leaf insects match the leaves of the plants they live on.

The skin of the **green moray eel** is actually blue-gray. This large predatory fish looks green because it is covered in a thick yellowish mucus that protects it against parasites. The green color that results also helps it hide among coral reefs and sea plants.

Blue and yellow make . . .

Common cuttlefish also use color to communicate. They seem to greet one another and exchange messages with a series of complex color changes.

The **three-toed sloth** is a gentle, slow-moving mammal that spends most of its life sleeping upside down in the trees of its rain forest home. The sloth's damp, shaggy fur is home to lots of bugs and moths. A special kind of algae (*al*-jee), a microscopic single-celled plant, also thrives on the sloth's hair. This algae gives the sloth's coat a green tint. In return for a place to live, it helps hide the sloth from hungry eagles and jaguars.

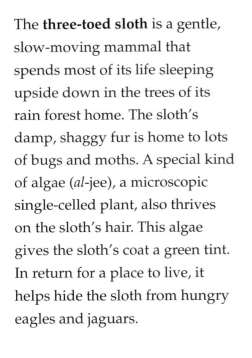

I don't *want* a bath.

I'm hiding in plain sight.

The **lesser green broadbill** is one of the most intensely colored birds in the world. In its native forest habitat, however, this little bird is hard to see among the bright green leaves.

Be green or be seen.

The **green anole** (uh-*noh*-lee), also called the American chameleon, is not really a chameleon. But it can change color, gradually turning different shades of green and brown to match its surroundings.

Here — no, over here.

The body of the **green tiger beetle** is a beautiful metallic green. This fierce predator is one of the fastest runners in the insect world. As it darts about on the ground, its metallic body seems to flash and change color, even disappearing at times. This makes it difficult for a predator to get a fix on it. Tiger beetles can also produce a bad-tasting substance if they are attacked.

It's really not my color.

I'm harmless.

Many poisonous caterpillars are brightly colored, and their appearance warns predators not to eat them. The **luna moth caterpillar** is harmless, however. Its color helps it stay hidden as it feeds on green plants.

The **giant green anemone** (uh-*nim*-uh-nee) looks like a flower, but it's actually a predatory animal with poisonous tentacles. It lives in shallow water and tidal pools found along rocky seacoasts. The anemone's body is colorless and transparent. Its tissues, however, are home to millions of green algae. These tiny plants help provide food and oxygen to the anemone. In return, the anemone gives the algae a place to live.

The delicate **leafy sea dragon** looks almost exactly like a bit of floating seaweed. It takes a very close look to realize that this relative of the seahorse is, in fact, a fish.

Look again . . .

. . . and again.

The **kelp isopod** (*eye*-suh-pod) is an air-breathing relative of the shrimp. It lives on the surface of the sea, scuttling about on floating blades of kelp, a kind of giant seaweed. The isopod's color helps it blend in and hide from hungry sea birds.

The **African chameleon** (kuh-*meel*-yun) changes color not to blend in with its surroundings but to express its emotions. A frightened, excited, or angry chameleon will change color to show other chameleons what it is feeling.

I'm very emotional.

Green

Orange says . . .

Back off.

The **garibaldi** (gar-uh-*bawl*-dee) lives in the cold waters of the Eastern Pacific. It lives near rocky sea floors and dense seaweed forests. It is unusual to find a brightly colored fish in this environment — most blend in with the dull rocks and blue-green plants. The garibaldi, however, defends its territory very aggressively and uses its color to warn other fish away.

The **orange pygmy seahorse** looks almost exactly like the tropical coral on which it makes its home. This little fish is not much bigger than your fingernail. When it hovers motionless in the water it is very difficult to see.

Colorful copy.

The male **African chameleon** also uses color to attract a mate and establish its territory.

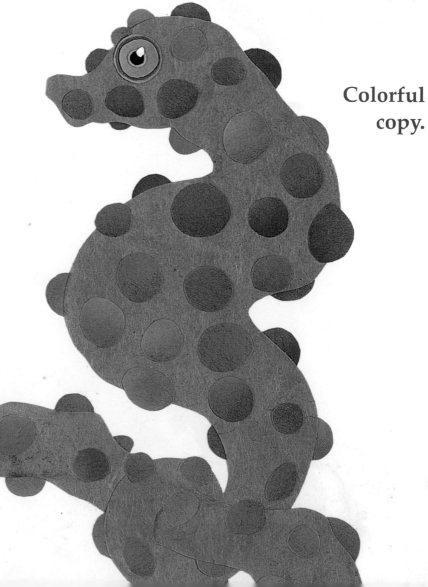

Better not eat me.

The caterpillar of the **monarch butterfly** feeds on the milkweed plant, which is poisonous to many animals. The butterfly's body absorbs this poison, so any bird or other animal that eats a monarch will become very sick. The insect's bright color warns predators that it is not good to eat.

Me either . . .

The **viceroy butterfly** is also toxic and tastes bad. It looks almost exactly like the monarch butterfly. Usually, a bird has to eat only one of a particular kind of insect to learn that it is foul-tasting. It helps these two butterflies to look so much alike, since either one can teach a predator an unpleasant lesson.

Make yourself at home.

The male **cock-of-the-rock** is one of the most colorful of all birds. It prepares and defends a special courting ground in the forest, called a lek (leck). Here, several male birds perform an elaborate dance, all competing for the attention of a single female. She will choose the male whose dance she likes best.

Real men dance.

The **leaf oyster** is camouflaged itself by a brightly colored sponge that grows on its shell. In the multicolored environment of a coral reef, this is a good disguise.

Purple says...

Move toward the light.

The **purple sea urchin** crawls about slowly on the sea floor, eating plants and decaying animals. Young sea urchins are green — they don't get their rich purple color until they are adults. The sharp spines of the sea urchin protect it and help it move around. The color of the spines probably helps warn away predators.

I'm full-grown and prickly.

The **deep-sea dragonfish** is about the length of a pencil, but the barbel growing from its chin can be as long as a full-grown man is tall. This dragonfish has a glowing purple light on the end of this whiplike filament and a row of glowing purple lights on either side of its body. In the total darkness of the deep ocean, these lights flash on and off to signal other dragonfish and attract prey.

What amphibian?

The **ringed caecilian** (see-*sil*-ee-uhn), a blind, burrowing amphibian, is a relative of the salamander. It looks like a huge purple earthworm. This shy creature leaves its burrow only at night. There is much we don't know about caecilians, but it may be that its purple color makes it difficult to detect in dim light.

I'm just a bunch of bubbles.

The **violet raft snail** blows a "raft" of sticky bubbles, using them to float along on the surface of the ocean. This snail is a predator, eating the tentacles of any jellyfish it bumps into. The bubbles and the snail's purple color protect it by making it look like a bit of drifting sea foam.

Which side is up?

The bodies of many ocean animals are dark on top and light on the bottom. This makes them hard to see from both above and below. The **blue sea slug** spends its life floating on its back, so it has the opposite color scheme — a dark purple belly (shown above) and a light blue back.

Impressive, isn't it?

The rare **long-wattled umbrella bird** is found only in a few remote South American rain forests. Its wattle, the long purple-black feathers that hang from its chest, makes flight difficult. This bird walks around on the forest floor, eating fruit and insects. It uses its amazing wattle to impress female umbrella birds.

Pink says...

I'm a boy now!

The teeth of the **parrotfish** have fused together, forming a tough, birdlike beak. This beak is strong enough to grind up rock-hard coral. Parrotfish eat the algae growing on the outside of the coral and the soft polyps living inside. The ground-up coral passes through the fish, coming out its other end as fine, powdery sand. Most female parrotfish are blue, green, or brown. If there are no males around, a female can change sex. The new male fish signals the change by turning bright pink, red, or yellow.

The **orchid mantis,** like its relative the praying mantis, is a fierce hunter. This beautifully camouflaged insect sits motionless inside a pink orchid, grabbing and eating any unlucky bee or butterfly that stops by.

Dressed to kill.

Turn off the light!

The **olm** is a rare, primitive amphibian. Found only in flooded caves in southern Europe, it is completely blind. Blood vessels inside the olm's body show through its colorless transparent skin, making it look pink.

Like the scarlet ibis, the **flamingo** gets its intense color from the food it eats — shrimp and other shellfish. Flamingos in zoos will eventually turn white if they don't eat enough shrimp or get special nutrients.

More shrimp, please.

There's no one home.
The **pink squat lobster** can often be found living inside a pink sponge on the sea floor. This lobster doesn't have a hard shell to protect it. It depends on its color and bristly, spongelike skin to help it hide from hungry predators.

Pretty in armor plating.
The **pink fairy armadillo** is small — it can rest comfortably in a person's hand. This little mammal's protective pink shell matches the color of the dry South American plains where it burrows, looking for ants and grubs to eat.

More about animal color . . .

For most animals, it's important to be able to see color. Almost all insects, amphibians, fish, reptiles, and birds have good color vision. They use color to send messages, hide, warn, mimic, or startle. Most of the animals in this book are just one color — they are mostly red, or blue, or yellow. Lots of other animals are a mixture of colors, or are dully colored with a brilliant patch or pattern. Many more, including most of the mammals, are shades of brown and gray — colors that blend in well with many environments.

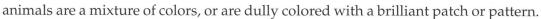

Why are mammals so drab?

With a few exceptions, mammals don't see color at all, or see a limited range of colors. Mammals have been around for more than 200 million years, but for most of this time they've been small creatures that were active at night. They were forced to hide from the reptiles, dinosaurs, and birds that dominated the earth, in turn, until about 40 million years ago. Color vision and brightly colored skin or fur doesn't make much sense for animals that come out only when it's dark. Humans and other primates — monkeys and apes — are among the few mammals that can see a wide range of colors. Perhaps we developed this ability when our tree-dwelling ancestors became active during the day. Color vision would have been very helpful as they searched for ripe fruit and tender young leaves and tried to avoid brightly colored snakes and spiders.

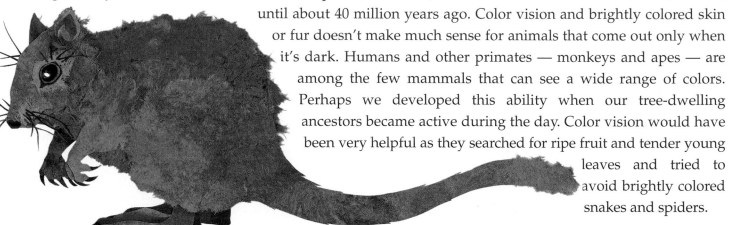

Rewarding but risky.

When an animal uses bright color to claim a territory or attract a mate, it also risks being noticed by a predator. Why do animals take this chance? In many species of animals, the female gets to choose her partner. Her choice is often based on the intensity of the male's skin or feathers, as well as the grace with which he presents his brilliant colors. This makes sense. Bright colors and a well-coordinated display show that he is strong and healthy and will help make babies that have a good chance of surviving.

Clever strategies.

Animals have worked out many ingenious solutions to the problem of attracting a mate but not a predator. Some lizards and birds are dully colored until they choose to display a hidden patch of bright skin or feathers. Some become vividly colored only for a short breeding season. Others, such as the chameleon, octopus, and cuttlefish, have come up with what may be the cleverest solution of all — they quickly change color at will, either to send a message or to hide from danger.

How is animal color created?

The science of animal color is complex, but there are two basic ways that animal color is created. The first relies on pigments to give skin, scales, feathers, or shells their color. Pigments are little colored particles — they are what make red paint red. In the animal world, pigments

are found in just three color families: brown-black, yellow-red, and white. The red of a salamander comes from a red pigment. Taken from the salamander's body, the pigment would still look red. The second kind of animal color is structural. Light reflected from or passing through an animal's feathers, scales, or skin is refracted, or scattered, in a way that makes it a particular color. The plumage of a blue bird doesn't actually contain anything blue. The color is created by the special way light is reflected from microscopic ridges on each feather. This is similar to the effect that creates the colors in a rainbow. Many animal colors are produced by a combination of pigments and structural colors. A green lizard, for instance, has a yellow pigment in its skin. It also refracts light that appears blue. This combination of yellow and blue make the lizard look green.

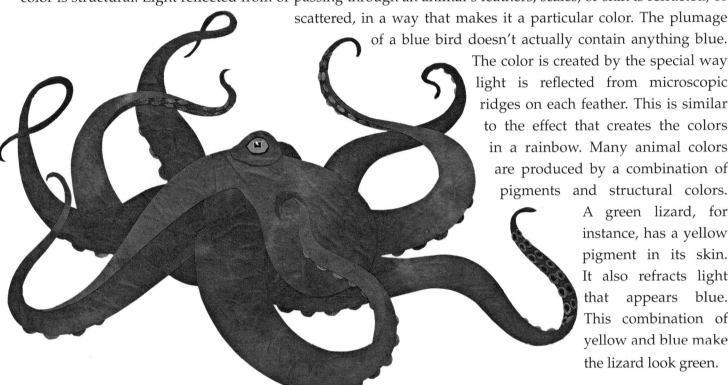

How do animal colors evolve?

When animals reproduce, the babies usually grow up to look like their parents. The offspring of two green frogs will, most of the time, become green frogs themselves. Occasionally, though, a different-looking frog is born. This can be caused by a mutation, the appearance of a trait that was not present in either parent. A mutation might result in a white or yellow frog being born. Most mutations make it harder for an animal to survive. A yellow frog will be probably easier for a bird or snake to spot, and it won't live very long. Sometimes, though, a mutation can be helpful. Perhaps the climate has been getting drier and there

are fewer green trees and more yellow grass in the frog's environment. In this case, the yellow frog might have a good chance of surviving and passing on its color to babies of its own. This process is called natural selection. It's the basis of evolution, and it is how new colors — and, eventually, new kinds of animals — appear. It is the reason there are so many different kinds of animals, and why they are found in so many different colors.

tomato frog

body length: up to 4 inches (10 centimeters)
habitat: pools and swamps in Madagascar
diet: insects, worms, small mammals

These amphibians sit in one spot and gobble up any prey that wanders within reach. They are endangered by the loss of their habitat and collectors who capture them to be sold as pets.

scarlet percher dragonfly

length: 1½ inches (38 millimeters)
habitat: ponds and streams in northeastern Australia
diet: flying insects

Dragonflies are serious predators. They are high-speed fliers with excellent eyesight and powerful jaws. They have lived on earth for 300 million years.

deep-sea jellyfish

bell diameter: up to 6 inches (15 centimeters)
habitat: oceans throughout the world
diet: algae and plankton (tiny animals)

There are many different kinds of deep-sea jellyfish. This one has a row of lights around its bell. A group of jellyfish is called a smack.

scarlet ibis (*eye*-bis)

length: 24 inches (61 centimeters)
habitat: seacoasts, rivers, and marshes in Central and South America
diet: shellfish, insects, worms, frogs

The male and female scarlet ibis are similar in appearance. They fly and roost in large flocks — a very colorful sight.

blood red fire shrimp

length: 2 inches (5 centimeters)
habitat: coral reefs in the Indo-Pacific (Eastern Indian and Southwestern Pacific oceans)
diet: fish parasites, dead fish and other animals

These shrimp are scavengers. They keep the reef clean by eating dead animals. They also clean live fish, removing parasites from their bodies.

Malaysian cherry-red centipede

length: 10 inches (25 centimeters)
habitat: in leaf litter, under rocks and logs in the forests in Southeast Asia
diet: insects, spiders, and other small animals

Centipedes are fast-moving and carnivorous. They use poisonous fangs to kill their prey. This centipede is large enough to eat the occasional lizard or mouse.

stonefish

length: 14 inches (36 centimeters)
habitat: shallow tropical seas in the Indo-Pacific Ocean
diet: fish and shrimp

When hunting, the stonefish waits until its prey swims close. Then it strikes with incredible speed. It lunges, opens its mouth wide, and sucks in its victim in a motion that's almost too fast to see.

hooded seal

length: males average 8 feet (2½ meters)
habitat: ice and deep water in the northern Atlantic Ocean
diet: fish and squid

These seals hunt deep under water and can hold their breath for fifty minutes. They make a pinging sound by shaking their inflated nasal sac back and forth.

flame scallop

width: 3 inches (7½ centimeters)
habitat: shallow coral reefs in the western Atlantic Ocean and Caribbean Sea
diet: algae and tiny animals filtered from the water

This mollusk can propel itself through the water by clapping the two halves of its shell together.

'i'iwi honeycreeper (ee-*ee*-wee)

length: 6 inches (15 centimeters)
habitat: mountainous tropical forests of Hawaii
diet: flower nectar, butterflies, and insects

The 'i'iwi's beak is perfectly shaped to reach into a flower and sip nectar. These birds produce a variety of squeaks and musical calls, and their wings make a buzzing sound as they fly through the forest.

white uakari (wah-*car*-ee)

length (head and body): 22 inches (56 centimeters)
habitat: swampy forests of Brazil and Peru
diet: fruit, seeds, flowers, and small animals

Uakaris live in groups of five to thirty animals. Both males and females have red faces, and the leaders of a group have the reddest faces. Bright color indicates a healthy monkey, making it more attractive to a mate.

red salamander

length: up to 7 inches (18 centimeters)
habitat: streams and forests in the eastern United States
diet: earthworms, insects, and spiders

Like all amphibians, salamanders live near water, laying their eggs in clear brooks and streams. They can often be found on land, but they spend the winter in the water.

harvest mite larva

length: 1/100 inch (¼ millimeter)
habitat: forests and grasslands around the world
diet: animal skin

A larva is a stage in the life of an animal that takes different forms as it grows up. A caterpillar, for example, is the larva of a butterfly. After a harvest mite grows up, it feeds on plant matter.

shield bug

length: ½ inch (1½ centimeters)
habitat: grasslands and forests throughout temperate and tropical parts of the world
diet: plant juices

There are many different kinds of shield bugs, also called stink bugs. The shield bug pictured lives in Southeast Asia.

crow

length: up to 20 inches (51 centimeters)
habitat: common throughout the world, found on every continent except South America and Antarctic
diet: fruit, seeds, eggs, carrion, insects, and small animals

Crows are one of the most intelligent birds. The mother crow lays three to eight eggs at a time, and both parents care for the young until they leave the nest at about five weeks of age.

hyacinth macaw (*hi*-ah-sinth muh-*caw*)

length: 39 inches (100 centimeters)
habitat: rain forests, forests and grasslands of Central and South America
diet: fruit, nuts, leaves, and insects

The hyacinth is the largest of the macaws. Their beaks, the strongest of any bird, are used to crack open tough nuts and fruit. Macaws can live for fifty years.

poison dart frog

length: 2 inches (5 centimeters)
habitat: rain forests of Central and South America
diet: ants, termites, beetles

There are many species of these small frogs, found in a variety of bright colors and patterns. All of them use color to warn off predators. Their distinctive skin also helps the frogs identify other members of their own species.

cleaner wrasse (*rass*)

length: 4 inches (10 centimeters)
habitat: coral reefs in the Indo-Pacific Ocean
diet: parasites (worms and crustaceans) and dead skin

These fish gather in a regular spot near a coral reef. Larger fish and turtles come to this "cleaning station" to have parasites removed from their skin, gills, and mouths.

robin's egg

length: 1 inch (2½ centimeters)
habitat: nests in trees and buildings throughout North America
diet: adult birds eat berries, worms, insects

This is the egg of the American robin. Female robins lay one egg each day, usually stopping when there are four in the nest. The eggs hatch in about two weeks.

blue morpho butterfly

wingspan: 6–8 inches (15–20 centimeters)
habitat: rain forests of Central and South America
diet: the juice of rotting fruit and fungi

The wings of this brilliant butterfly do not contain any blue coloring. The tops of the wings are covered with tiny scales that refract light in a way that makes them appear blue.

cobalt blue tarantula

leg span: up to 5 inches (13 centimeters)
habitat: silk-lined burrows in the tropical forests of Southeast Asia
diet: insects, small lizards and amphibians

These spiders are shy, quick, and aggressive. Their bite is painful to humans, but not deadly.

blue-winged grasshopper

length: 1 inch (2½ centimeters)
habitat: dry open areas of Europe and Northern Africa
diet: leaves and grass

Males make a faint noise by rubbing their legs together. These insects are very hard to see when they sit motionless on dirt or dry plants.

Portuguese man-of-war

body length: up to 12 inches (30 centimeters)
tentacle length: up to 165 feet (50 meters)
habitat: warm seas throughout the world
diet: fish, squid, shrimp, plankton

These beautiful but dangerous animals are colonies of four kinds of polyps (*pol*-ips) — thousands of tiny simple animals that live together. Each kind of polyp does a different job: floating, stinging, digesting, or reproducing. Man-of-war stings can be painful, even fatal, to humans.

blue bird of paradise

length: 12 inches (30 centimeters)
habitat: mountainous forests of New Guinea
diet: fruit and insects

These beautiful birds are threatened by the loss of their forest habitat to farming and logging. In the past, many birds of paradise were killed for their feathers, which were used to decorate women's hats.

blue-tongued skink

length: up to 24 inches (61 centimeters)
habitat: grasslands and forests of eastern Australia
diet: fruit, flowers, insects, worms, and snails

Most lizards are hatched from eggs, but these reptiles are born alive, six to twelve at a time. They can live up to twenty years.

blue-tailed skink

length: up to 10 inches (25 centimeters)
habitat: tropical and temperate areas throughout the world
diet: insects and spiders

There are several species of skinks with blue tails found in different parts of the world. They all use their tails to distract predators in the same way.

crab spider

length (female): ⅜ inch (1 centimeter)
habitat: yellow or white flowers in fields and gardens throughout North America
diet: bees, wasps, moths, and butterflies

These spiders will remain in the same spot for days or weeks, waiting for prey. They get their name from their crablike sideways movement.

Madagascar moon moth

length: 7 inches (18 centimeters)
habitat: rain forests of Madagascar

This insect does all its eating as a caterpillar. The adult moth has no mouth and cannot eat, and lives only about ten days.

yellow mongoose

length: 20 inches (50 centimeters)
habitat: dry scrubland in southern Africa
diet: insects, lizards, eggs, small mammals

These mammals live in colonies in complex underground burrows. Their color helps hide them from their predators — eagles, snakes, and jackals.

trumpet fish

average length: 24 inches (60 centimeters)
diet: fish and shrimp
habitat: coral reefs in tropical seas worldwide

This fish is a relative of the seahorse. There are many different species of trumpet fish. They vary in size, but they all hunt the same way, using a technique known as "lurk and lunge."

great hornbill

length: 63 inches (160 centimeters)
wingspan: 60 inches (152 centimeters)
habitat: forest in India, China, and Southeast Asia
diet: fruit, but also snakes, lizards, and small mammals

After mating, the female hornbill finds a hole in a tree, climbs inside, and seals the opening with a mixture of dirt, bark, and her droppings. She leaves a small hole through which the male can give her food. She will stay inside until her eggs hatch, about forty days later.

eyelash viper

length: up to 30 inches (76 centimeters)
habitat: wet forests in Central and South America
diet: small mammals, lizards, frogs, and birds

This snake gets its name from an enlarged scale above each eye. It is not aggressive, but it will bite if it is touched. The viper's poison is dangerous to humans, causing pain and sometimes death.

yellow crazy ant

length: ⅕ inch (5 millimeters)
habitat: cities and agricultural land in warm climates around the world
diet: insects, small amphibians, reptiles, mammals, and other small animals

Crazy ants don't bite, but if people get the ants' acid spray on their hands and rub their eyes, injury or blindness can result.

yellow crab

width: 4 inches (10 centimeters)
habitat: tropical forest leaf litter, usually near a coastline
diet: decaying plant material, dead animals

Many different species of land crabs are found across the world. Some are yellow, others are red, black, white, brown, or purple. Land crabs feed on plant debris and help keep the forest floor clean.

ladybird beetle

length: ¼ inch (6 millimeters)
habitat: fields and gardens in temperate parts of Asia, Europe, and North America
diet: aphids and other soft-bodied insects

There are thousands of different kinds of ladybird beetles. The yellow beetle pictured is an Asian ladybird beetle. People release these insects in their gardens to eat aphids, tiny insects that suck the juice from plants.

American goldfinch

length: 5 inches (13 centimeters)
habitat: fields, orchards, and gardens throughout the United States, southern Canada, and northern Mexico
diet: mostly seeds, some insects

During the fall and winter, when it is not trying to attract a mate, this bird's brilliant feathers turn a dull brown.

common cuttlefish

length: 18 inches (45 centimeters)
habitat: coastal waters of the eastern Atlantic Ocean and the Mediterranean Sea
diet: shellfish, crabs, shrimp, fish

The cuttlefish is a relative of the octopus and squid. It moves by jet propulsion, pushing water out of a tube on the bottom of its body. It can also squirt brown ink into the water to confuse predators.

leaf insect

average length: 3½ inches (9 centimeters)
habitat: forests of Southeast Asia and Australia
diet: leaves

There are about twenty-five different kinds of leaf insect. Each looks like a different plant. Most are a reddish color when they hatch and turn green after they begin to eat plants.

green moray eel

length: up to 8 feet (2½ meters)
habitat: warm, shallow waters of the western Atlantic Ocean
diet: fish, squid, crabs, and shrimp

Morays lurk in rock and coral crevices. Because these fish can deliver a nasty bite, human divers should be wary of them.

three-toed sloth

length: up to 30 inches (76 centimeters)
habitat: rain forests of Central and South America
diet: leaves and buds

Sloths sleep about fifteen hours a day and move very slowly. If attacked, however, they fight fiercely with their long, sharp claws. Sloths are also good swimmers.

lesser green broadbill

length: 6 inches (15 centimeters)
habitat: rain forests of Southeast Asia
diet: figs and other fruit, seeds

Because people are destroying their rain forest habitat, these brilliant birds are becoming increasingly rare.

green anole (uh-*noh*-lee)

length: 8 inches (20 centimeters)
habitat: coastal areas of the southeastern United States and Caribbean islands
diet: insects, worms, flower nectar

Some people keep anoles as pets. They can change color from green to brown to match their surroundings. Changes in temperature and mood can also cause their color to shift.

green tiger beetle

length: ⅝ inches (1½ centimeters)
habitat: open woodlands and fields throughout the world
diet: ants, spiders, other insects

Tiger beetles get their name from their fierce hunting behavior. They use their huge eyes to spot prey and avoid predators.

luna moth caterpillar

length: 3 inches (7½ centimeters)
habitat: eastern North America
diet: tree leaves

This caterpillar is the larva of a large, night-flying moth with green wings that can span 4½ inches (11½ centimeters). The adult moths do not eat — their only task is to reproduce. They live only about a week.

giant green anemone (uh-*nim*-uh-*nee*)

diameter: up to 9 inches (23 centimeters)
habitat: costal waters of the northeastern Pacific Ocean
diet: mussels, crabs, small fish

Some fish, their bodies covered in protective mucus, can swim safely among the anemone's poison tentacles. The anemone can be found above the water at low tide, stuck fast to a rock and closed up tightly so they don't dry out.

leafy sea dragon

length: up to 18 inches (46 centimeters)
habitat: kelp beds in ocean waters south and west of Australia
diet: tiny shrimp and other animals

The male sea dragon has a special patch of skin on his belly. Here he carries the eggs his female partner lays, until they hatch.

kelp isopod

(*eye*-suh-pod)

length: 1 ½ inches (4 centimeters)
habitat: kelp beds in the northeastern Pacific Ocean
diet: kelp and other kinds of algae

Kelp isopods are relatives of the more familiar pill bug, or roly-poly.

African chameleon

length: 12 inches (30 centimeters)
habitat: forest and shrublands of Africa and Madagascar
diet: mostly insects, small birds

There are about one hundred different kinds of chameleons. All can change color and have a long, sticky tongue that is shot out to capture prey. Since they can move each eye independently, chameleons can look in two different directions at the same time.

garibaldi

length: 14 inches (36 centimeters)
habitat: reefs, rocky sea bottoms, and kelp forests in the northeastern Pacific Ocean
diet: shrimp, crabs, and small animals

When there are not enough males or females in a group, these colorful fish can change sex to balance things out. The same fish can change back and forth many times.

orange pygmy seahorse

length: ¾ inch (2 centimeters)
habitat: orange coral in shallow waters of the southwestern Pacific Ocean
diet: tiny shrimp and plankton

This tiny fish lives on just one kind of coral, an orange sea fan.

monarch butterfly

length: 4 ½ inches (11½ centimeters)
habitat: meadows, fields, and marshes in most warm parts of the world
diet: caterpillars eat only milkweed plants; adults eat flower nectar

Monarchs in North America make an 1,800-mile (2,900-kilometer) journey from Canada and the northeastern United States to Mexico every winter, returning the next spring. A single butterfly does not live long enough to complete the trip. It is the grandchild of a monarch that leaves Mexico in the spring that makes it back the next winter.

viceroy butterfly

wingspan: 3 inches (8 centimeters)
habitat: meadows and marshes throughout most of North America
diet: flower nectar, animal droppings, and the juices of dead animals

This butterfly looks almost exactly like the monarch, except for a black line that runs across its lower wings.

cock-of-the-rock

length: up to 10 inches (25 centimeters)
habitat: mountainous rain forests of northern South America
diet: primarily fruit, some insects

These tropical birds often make their nests on the sides of cliffs. The females are brown, and much less colorful than the males. Since they aren't as easily seen, it's safer for them to stay on their nests and raise their young.

leaf oyster

length: up to 4 inches (10 centimeters)
habitat: shallow waters in the southwestern Pacific Ocean
diet: algae and plankton filtered from the water

Many oysters living in the same area create a habitat called an oyster reef. It is similar to a coral reef. The oyster shells make a home for anemones and other animals, and attract fish. All oysters begin life as males. Later they change sex, and most end up as females.

purple sea urchin

length: up to 3 inches (7½ centimeters)
habitat: Pacific Ocean waters off the western coast of North America
diet: dead plant and animal matter

Sea urchins use their spines to move along the bottom of the ocean. If touched, they point their spines in the direction of a possible attack. They also use their spines to dig protective holes in soft rock.

deep-sea dragonfish

length: 6 inches (15 centimeters)
habitat: deep tropical waters around the world
diet: fish and squid

These fish live at depths of up to 5,000 feet (1,500 meters). Here there is no sunlight, just the dim glow of luminescent animals.

ringed caecilian (see-*sil*-ee-uhn)

length: 14 inches (35 centimeters)
habitat: burrows in the rain forests of South America
diet: worms, insects, frogs, and other small animals

The caecilian uses its blunt head as a ramrod to push its way through the earth. There are well over one hundred different species of caecilian. Some are no larger than an earthworm, while others grow to be 5 feet (1 ½ meters) long.

violet raft snail

width: 1 ½ inches (4 centimeters)
habitat: tropical and subtropical waters worldwide
diet: jellyfish and Portuguese man-of-war tentacles

This snail spends its life on the open ocean. It drifts with the wind, feeding when it bumps into a jellyfish. Sometimes a storm will wash millions of raft snails up onto the beach, creating a fantastic purple landscape.

blue sea slug

length: 1 ½ inches (4 centimeters)
habitat: warm ocean waters throughout the world
diet: Portugese man-of-war tentacles

These slugs sometimes wash onto the beach, where they can give a painful sting to anyone who touches them.

long-wattled umbrella bird

length: 18 inches (46 centimeters)
wattle: 11 inches (28 centimeters) long
habitat: mountainous rain forests in South America
diet: fruit, insects, frogs, and small lizards

The male umbrella birds performs a special display to impress a female. He inflates his wattle, spreads the crest of feathers on his head, and makes a low rumbling noise.

parrotfish

length: up to 3 feet (91 centimeters)
habitat: shallow reefs in warm oceans worldwide
diet: algae, coral polyps

Each night, the parrotfish secretes and sleeps inside a mucous cocoon. This slimy coating masks their odor and protects them from predators.

orchid mantis

length (female): 4½ inches (11 centimeters)
habitat: rain forests of Southeast Asia
diet: flying insects, small lizards

The male is about half the size of the female. Like the black widow spider, the female will often kill and eat the male after mating. This meal gives her a better chance of surviving to lay eggs — it's the reason the male lets himself be eaten.

olm

length: up to 12 inches (30 centimeters)
habitat: flooded caves in southern Europe
diet: worms and crayfish

The olm is rare and endangered by pollution. Its unseeing eyes are covered by skin, so it finds its prey with a good sense of smell and the ability to detect slight vibrations. Olms may live for more than fifty years.

flamingo

height: up to 5 feet (1½ meters)
habitat: shallow lakes, marshes, and lagoons in many tropical areas of the world
diet: water plants and shellfish

When it feeds, the flamingo lowers its head upside down and takes a mouthful of muddy water. Its big tongue pushes the water past the rough edges of its bill, and algae and small animals are trapped in its mouth and swallowed.

pink squat lobster

length: 1½ inches (4 centimeters)
habitat: coral reefs in the southwestern Pacific Ocean
diet: algae, plankton, and other bits of animal matter

These tiny animals are not really lobsters but are more closely related to hermit crabs. Their delicate bodies are covered with bristly hairs.

pink fairy armadillo

length: 4 inches (10 centimeters)
habitat: sandy plains and grasslands of southern South America
diet: ants, other insects, and worms

The smallest of the armadillos, this shy nocturnal creature is endangered by the loss of its habitat to growing cities and farms.

For Jamie

The text of this book is set in Palatino.
The illustrations are cut-paper collage.

The Library of Congress has cataloged the hardcover edition as follows:
Jenkins, Steve, 1952–
Living color / written and illustrated by Steve Jenkins.
p. cm.

1. Animals—Color—Juvenile literature. I. Title.
QL767.J46 2007   591.47'2-dc22

2007012751

ISBN 978-0-618-70897-0 hardcover
ISBN 978-0-547-57682-4 paperback

Manufactured in China
LEO 10 9 8 7 6 5 4 3 2 1

4500325420

To learn more about animal color:

Animals and Their Colors: Camouflage, Warning Coloration, Courtship and Territorial Display, Mimicry.
By Michael and Patricia Fogden.
Crown Publishers, 1974.

Animal Dazzlers: The Role of Brilliant Colors in Nature.
By Sneed B. Collard III.
Franklin Watts, 1998.

Dramatic Displays.
By Tim Knight.
Heinemann Library, 2003.

Red Eyes or Blue Feathers: A Book About Animal Colors.
By Patricia M. Stockland,
illustrated by Todd Ouren.
Picture Window Books, 2005.